Postman Pat®

Ted Glen

SIMON AND SCHUSTER

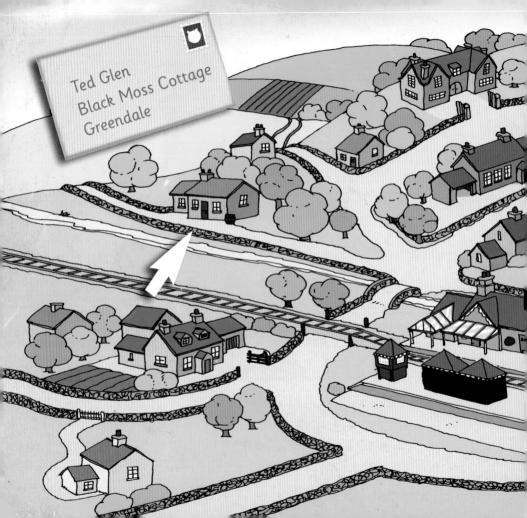

Ted Glen
Black Moss Cottage
Greendale

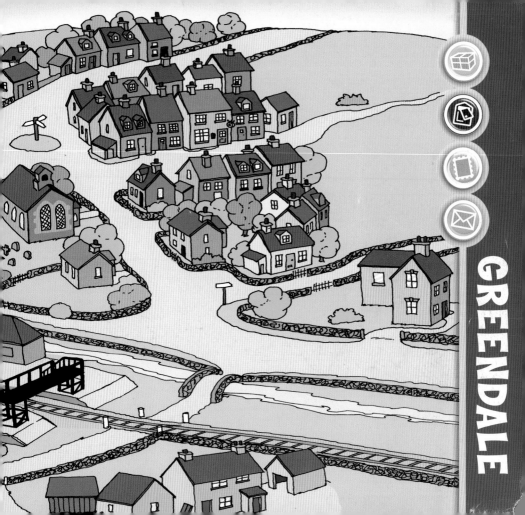

GREENDALE

Come and say hello to Ted Glen!

Ted is the local handyman, always ready to oil a squeaky gate or replace a broken window. But Ted doesn't just fix things. Sometimes he invents brand new devices to help his Greendale friends . . .

Ted was busy tinkering in his workshop.

"Parcel for you!" smiled Pat, knocking on the door. He'd brought his son, Julian, on the round today.

Ted looked up and grinned. "I reckon I know what that might be."

"Can we watch you open it?" asked Julian.

Jess padded up to Ted. Even he wanted to see what was inside!

Ted let Julian tear open the brown paper. Inside was a shiny new drill.

"I've been after this for weeks," Ted explained. "What a beauty!"

"I'd better leave you to it," waved Pat. "There's lots of post to deliver today."

"OK Pat," he said. "But perhaps Julian would like to stay and help me try this out?"

"I'm sure he would, Ted!" said Pat.

When Pat and Jess had gone, Ted carefully unpacked his drill, while Julian read out the instructions.

"Bet you can't wait to use it!" said Julian.

Ted nodded. "She's a grand bit of machinery."

"So what are you going to use it for first?"

Suddenly Ted was stumped. There wasn't a single job on his list that needed any drilling!

"By gum, I've got it!" Ted cried at last.

Julian leapt off his stool. "What's the plan?"

"We're going to build a delivery machine to help your dad on his rounds," he announced proudly.

Julian wasn't too sure. "Um . . ."

"No time for 'ums', lad," said Ted. "We've got to get busy!"

By lunchtime, they were on their way to Forge Cottage.

"Ta-da!" cried Ted, placing his invention on the dining-room table.

"It's for you, Dad," whispered Julian.

Pat stared at the strange device. "I don't know what to say."

"This machine delivers letters without you stepping out of the van!" Ted explained.

Pat agreed to give the Delivery Machine a try the next morning.

"Here goes, Jess," he sighed, as they pulled up outside Dr Gilbertson's house.

Pat loaded the machine up then pressed the remote control. The machine's arm stretched down the path and delivered the mail in seconds.

"Hmmm . . . at this rate, we'll be done in no time!"

When Pat and Jess got back to the Post Office, Ted was waiting for them.

"By 'eck, you're an hour early!" he cried.

Pat nodded, then frowned down at Jess.

Ted couldn't help noticing how glum they both looked.

"Uh-oh! Did it go wrong?" he asked.

"Not once," said Pat. "In fact, it worked too well."

Pat explained that with the machine doing all the work, he never got to talk to anybody.

"It's a big part of my job to say hello to the villagers," he said.

Ted gulped. "I hadn't thought of that."

Suddenly Alf Thompson tapped him on the shoulder. "So does that mean I could borrow that device of yours?"

Alf asked everyone to follow him back to Thompson Ground.

"Your machine will be just the thing for picking the apples in my orchard," he explained.

Ted got started straight away.

"Thank you, Ted," smiled Dorothy Thompson. "I'll make sure you're well paid in apple pies."

"I'm just glad to be of service!" Ted beamed. "All those hours spent in my workshop weren't fruitless, after all!"

SIMON AND SCHUSTER
First published in 2005 in Great Britain by Simon & Schuster UK Ltd
Africa House, 64-78 Kingsway, London WC2B 6AH

Postman Pat® © 2005 Woodland Animations, a division of Entertainment Rights PLC
Licensed by Entertainment Rights PLC
Original writer John Cunliffe
From the original television design by Ivor Wood
Royal Mail and Post Office imagery is used by kind permission of Royal Mail Group plc
All rights reserved

Illustrations by Baz Rowell © 2005 Simon & Schuster UK Ltd
Text by Mandy Archer © 2005 Simon & Schuster UK Ltd

A CIP catalogue record for this book is available from the British Library upon request

ISBN 1416901817
Printed in China

1 3 5 7 9 10 8 6 4 2